Here I

Susan Meyers

Illustrated by Susan Lexa

milk
cheese
bread
juice
jam
corn
ice cream

Rigby®

A Harcourt Achieve Imprint

www.Rigby.com
1-800-531-5015

We look for milk.

"Here it is!" said Marta.

We look for cheese.
"Here it is!" said Marta.

We look for bread.
"Here it is!" said Marta.

6

We look for juice.
"Here it is!" said Marta.

We look for jam.
"Here it is!" said Marta.

We look for corn.
"Here it is!" said Marta.

13

We look for ice cream.

"Here it is!" said Marta.